ألف ليلة و ليلة

للمبتدئين في تعلم العربية المصرية

One Thousand and One Nights

for Elementary Egyptian Arabic
Language Learners

lingualism

© 2023 by Matthew Aldrich

The author's moral rights have been asserted. All rights reserved. No part of this document may be reproduced or transmitted in any form or by any means, electronic, mechanical, photocopying, recording, or otherwise, without prior written permission of the publisher.

ISBN: 978-1-949650-92-1

Conceptualized by Matthew Aldrich

Written by Ahmad Al-Masri

Edited by Hend Khaled and Matthew Aldrich

Illustrations by Duc-Minh Vu

Audio by Mohamed Shehata

website: www.lingualism.com

email: contact@lingualism.com

Table of Contents

II .... INTRODUCTION

V .... HOW TO USE THIS BOOK

1 .... الفَصْل الأوّل: الوَزير و بِنْته و المَلِك
        Chapter 1: The Vizier, His Daughter, and the King

8 .... الفَصْل الثّاني: الجِنّي و التّاجِر
        Chapter 2: The Genie and the Merchant

17 .... الفَصْل الثّالِث: الصَّيّاد و السَّمكة الذَّهبية
        Chapter 3: The Fisherman and the Golden Fish

25 .... الفَصْل الرّابِع: علاء الدّين و المِصْباح السِّحْري
        Chapter 4: Aladdin and the Magic Lamp

34 .... الفَصْل الخامِس: علي بابا و الأَرْبعين حرامي
        Chapter 5: Ali Baba and the Forty Thieves

41 .... الفَصْل السّادِس: الفَلّاح الذَّكي و الجِنّي الشَّقي
        Chapter 6: The Clever Farmer and the Mischievous Genie

49 .... الفَصْل السّابِع: حرامي إسْكَنْدِرية و رَئيس الشُّرْطة
        Chapter 7: The Thief of Alexandria and the Police Chief

57 .... الفَصْل الثّامِن: العُصْفور الأَزْرق
        Chapter 8: The Blue Bird

65 .... الفَصْل التّاسِع: البِنْت و السّاحِرة العجوزة
        Chapter 9: The Girl and the Magical Old Woman

72 .... الفَصْل العاشِر: الأَمير و التِّنين
        Chapter 10: The Prince and the Dragon

Introduction

"One Thousand and One Nights for Elementary Egyptian Arabic Language Learners" is a captivating anthology designed specifically for adult Arabic language learners at the elementary level. This unique collection features the cherished classic tales in a simplified, yet engaging format, making it an excellent resource for those venturing into the enchanting world of Arabic language and literature.

The book comes with an array of special features to ensure an immersive and effective learning experience:

- **Diacritics for Pronunciation:** We've included diacritical marks (tashkeel) in the Arabic text to assist you in correct pronunciation, and to clarify the meaning of the words, easing your reading experience.

- **Professional Audio Accompaniment:** The book is supplemented with high-quality, slow-paced audio readings by a professional voice artist who is a native Arabic speaker from Egypt. This allows you to listen and mimic the correct pronunciation, intonation, and rhythm of Egyptian Arabic.

- **Comprehension Questions and Answers:** Each chapter is followed by a set of comprehension questions, along with their answers. This interactive feature helps to reinforce your understanding of the story and the language constructs used within it.

- **English Translations:** To support your learning, we've provided English translations of the stories. These can be used as a reference to cross-check your understanding of the Arabic text.

All these features work together to provide a comprehensive and enriching learning experience, ensuring you make consistent progress in your Arabic language journey.

The tales in this book have been carefully curated and reimagined to match the language proficiency of elementary-level learners. We have incorporated level-appropriate vocabulary throughout the stories, ensuring you are neither overwhelmed by complexity nor left unchallenged. To enhance memorization and recognition, we've deliberately woven repetitive patterns of phrases and language structures into the text, encouraging natural language acquisition and recall.

Each chapter is short, and perfectly crafted to be absorbed in a single sitting, allowing you to steadily build your comprehension skills and vocabulary without feeling rushed. The stories retain the intrigue and charm of the original tales, providing you with a sense of accomplishment and enjoyment as you navigate your way through each tale.

Once you've mastered the stories and vocabulary in this book, we invite you to progress to the "One Thousand and One Nights for Intermediate Egyptian Arabic Language Learners." In this next step of your language journey, you'll find the same beloved stories, but presented in slightly different versions. These alternate renditions are imbued with greater detail, building on the vocabulary you learn in this book, and introducing you to new vocabulary and more nuanced language structures. This ensures a smooth, seamless transition towards more advanced language learning.

With "One Thousand and One Nights for Elementary Egyptian Arabic Language Learners," not only will you embark on a remarkable journey through some of the most enchanting stories ever told, but you'll also be laying a strong and solid foundation for your Arabic language learning adventure.

How to Use This Book

"One Thousand and One Nights for Elementary Egyptian Arabic Language Learners" has been designed to offer flexibility to adapt to your individual learning style. Here's how you can utilize the features of the book according to your needs:

1. **Choose Your Approach:** You have the freedom to approach the stories in multiple ways. You could begin by tackling the Arabic text first, immersing yourself in the structure of the language and the flow of the story. Alternatively, you could start by listening to the accompanying audio, to attune your ear to the sound and rhythm of Egyptian Arabic. This can be particularly helpful if you are a more auditory learner.
2. **Use English Translations:** If you're finding the Arabic text or audio challenging, you can refer to the English translations to aid your understanding. Over time, as your comprehension improves, you could challenge yourself by attempting to read or listen to the Arabic without relying on the translations.
3. **Engage with Questions:** You can choose to tackle the comprehension questions before or after reading the story. Attempting them beforehand can provide a focus for your reading, while answering them after

allows you to assess your understanding of the text. Remember, the answers provided in the book are examples and your own answers, while differently worded, may still be correct.

4. **Repetition and Practice:** This book has been designed to promote repetition and practice, key strategies for language learning. We encourage you to revisit chapters and listen to the audio multiple times to reinforce your understanding and memorization.

Remember, the most effective learning strategy is the one that works best for you. So don't be afraid to experiment with different approaches until you find what suits you best.

Visit www.lingualism.com/audio, where you can find the free accompanying audio to download or stream (at variable playback rates).

الفَصْل الأوّل
الوَزير و بِنْتُه و المَلِك

في يوْم مِن الأيّام، في بلد بِعيدة، كان فيه ملِك حكيم و عادِل إسْمُه شهْرَيار. كان بيُحْكُم ممْلكة كِبيرة، و شعْبُه كان بيْحِبُّه جِدّاً.

في قصْر الملِك، كان فيه راجِل حكيم إسْمُه جعْفر و كان هُوَّ الوَزير. كان بيْساعِد الملِك في القرارات المُهِمّة. جعْفر كان راجِل طيِّب و

مُخْلِص، و كان عنْدُه بِنْت جميلة إسْمها شهْرزاد.

شهْرزاد كانِت بِنْت ذكية و شُجاعة. كانِت بِتْحِبّ تِقْرا و تِتْعلّم حاجات عن الدُّنْيا. كانِت بِتِعْرف قِصص كِتير و بِتِعْرف تِحْكيها بِطريقة تِخلّي النّاس تِحِبّ تِسْمعْها.

في يوْم مِن الأيّام، قرّر الملِك شهْرَيار إنُّه عايِز يِتْجوّز. طلب مِن وَزيرُه يِدوّرْلُه على عروسة. دوّر جعْفر كِتير بسّ معْرِفْش يِلاقي عروسة مُناسِبة لِلْملِك.

فجْأة، خطرِت فِكْرة لِشهْرزاد. راحِت لأبوها الوَزير و قالِتْلُه: "يا والْدي، أنا عايْزة أبْقى مِراةْ الملِك. أنا عنْدي قِصص كِتير أحْكيهالُه. و أقْدر أسْعِدُه."

الوَزير كان قلْقان على بِنْتُه. كان عارِف إنّ الملِك شهْرَيار مُمْكِن يِغْضب ساعات. بسّ شهْرزاد كانِت مُصمِّمة إنّها تِتْجوِّز الملِك.

و عشان كِده، وافِق الوَزير على الجَواز. و قال لِلْملِك شهْرَيار على بِنْتُه،

و الملِك وافِق يِتْجوِّزْها.

في ليْلة فرحْهُمْ، بدأِتْ شهْرزاد تِحْكي لِلْملِك قِصّة. كانِت القِصّة حِلْوَة أَوي لِدرجِةْ إنّ الملِك كان عايِزْها تِحْكيلُه قِصص كمان. قالِتْلُه شهْرزاد: "أنا هكمِّل القِصّة بُكْره باللّيْل لَوْ هتِسمحْلي." وافِق الملِك شهْرَيار على طلَبها، و كان عايِز يِسْمع قِصص كمان و كمان.

و بِكِده، بدأِت شهْرزاد تِحْكي القِصص لِلْملِك شهْرَيار كُلّ ليْلة. كانِت القِصص ملْيانة مُغامْرات و غُموض و حُبّ. كان الملِك مُتحمِّس إنُّه يِسْمع كُلّ قِصّة جِديدة و كان بيِتْعلِّم مِنْها حاجات كتير عن الحَياة و الدُّنْيا.

Questions

1. أيْه إسْمِ الملِك الحكيم العادِل؟

2. أيْه الحاجة اللي كانِت شهْرزاد بِتْحِبّ تِعْمِلْها؟

3. أيْه اللي طلبُه الملِك شهْرَيار مِن وَزيرُه جعْفر؟

4. إزّاي شهْرزاد اِتْعرّفِت على الملِك شهْرَيار؟

5. أيْه الحاجة اللي بدأِت شهْرزاد تِعْمِلْها كُلّ ليْلة بعْد ما اتْجوِّزِت الملِك شهْرَيار؟

Answers

1. إسْم الملِك هُوَّ شهْرَيار.

2. كانِت شهْرزاد بِتْحِبّ تِقْرا و تِتْعلّم حاجات عن الدُّنْيا، و كانت بِتِعْرف قِصص كِتير، و بِتِعْرف تحْكيها.

3. طلب الملِك شهْرَيار مِن وَزيرُه جعْفر إنُّه يِدوّرْلُه على عروسة.

4. راحِت شهْرزاد لِأبوها الوَزير و قالِتْلُه إنّها عايْزة تِبْقى مِراةْ الملِك، و بعْديْن الوَزير قال لِلْملِك على بِنْتُه و الملِك وافِق إنُّه بِتْجوّزْها.

5. بدإِت شهْرزاد تِحْكي قِصص لِلْملِك شهْرَيار كُلّ ليْلة.

Chapter 1: The Vizier, His Daughter, and the King

Once upon a time, in a faraway land, there was a wise and just king named Shahryar. He ruled a great kingdom and was loved by his people.

In the king's court, there was a wise man named Ja'far, who was the vizier. He helped the king make important decisions. Ja'far was a kind and loyal man, and he had a beautiful daughter named Scheherazade.

Scheherazade was a intelligent, brave girl. She loved reading and learning about the world. She knew many stories and could tell them in a way that made people listen.

One day, King Shahryar decided that he needed a queen. He asked his vizier to find him a wife. Ja'far searched for a long time but could not find a suitable wife for the king.

Scheherazade had an idea. She went to her father, the vizier, and said, "Father, I want to be the king's wife. I have many stories to tell him. I can make him happy."

The vizier was worried about his daughter. He knew that King Shahryar could get very angry sometimes. But Scheherazade was determined to marry the king.

So the vizier agreed to the marriage. He told King Shahryar about his daughter, and the king agreed to marry her.

On their wedding night, Scheherazade began to tell the king a story. The story was so interesting that the king wanted to hear more. Scheherazade said, "I will finish the story tomorrow night if you allow me." King Shahryar agreed and wanted to hear more stories.

And so Scheherazade began to tell stories to King Shahryar every night. The stories were full of adventures, mysteries, and love. The king was eager to hear every new story and learned a lot about life and the world from them.

Questions
1. What is the name of the wise and just king?
2. What did Scheherazade love to do?
3. What did King Shahryar ask his vizier Ja'far to do?
4. How did Scheherazade meet King Shahryar?
5. What did Scheherazade begin to do every night after marrying King Shahryar?

Answers
1. The name of the king is Shahryar.
2. Scheherazade loved reading and learning about the world, and she knew many stories that she could tell.
3. King Shahryar asked his vizier Ja'far to find him a wife.
4. Scheherazade went to her father, the vizier, and said she wanted to be the king's wife, so the vizier told the king about his daughter, and the king agreed to marry her.
5. Scheherazade began to tell stories to King Shahryar every night.

الفَصْل التّاني
الجِنّي و التّاجِر

في اللّيْلة اللي بعْدها، طلب الملِك شهْرَيار مِن شهْرزاد إنّها تِحْكيلُه قِصّة جِديدة. فا بدأتِ شهْرزاد تِحْكي قِصّة التّاجِر و الجِنّي العجيب.

في يوْم مِن الأيّام، سافِر تاجِر غني في رِحْلة بِعيدة علشان يِبيع بِضاعْتُه. بعْد رِحْلة طَويلة و مُتْعِبة، وقِف التّاجِر علشان يِسْتريّح تحْتَ

شجرة. و هُوَّ قاعِد هُناك، ظهر جِنّي عِمْلاق و غضبان.

قال الجِنّي لِلتّاجِر: "أنا هقْتِلك علشان إنْتَ دمّرْت بيْتى." التّاجِر كان خايِف و مِش فاهِم الجِنّي يُقْصُد أيْه. طلب مِن الجِنّي يِفهِّمُه هُوَّ ليْه زعْلان.

فا ردّ الجِنّي: "لمّا إنْتَ جيْت و شِلْت الجِذْع الخشب ده علشان تُقْعُد عليْه، وَقّعْت عليّا حاجات و دمّرْت بيْتى الصُّغيّر اللي كُنْت عايِش فيه."

كان التّاجِر زعْلان بِسبب اللي حصل، بسّ هُوَّ مكانش عارِف إنّ فيه بيْت جِنّي وَرا الشّجرة. طلب مِن الجِنّي إنُّه يِكون رحيم و يِسامْحُه.

قال الجِنّي: "أنا هدّيك فُرْصة تِجيب حدّ يِقْنِعْني إنّي مقْتِلكْش. لَوْ فشِلْت، أكيد هقْتِلك."

راح التّاجِر في رِحْلة طَويلة يِدوّر على حدّ يِساعْدُه. في النِّهايَة، لِقي راجِل عجوز حكيم كان بيِعْرف حاجات كتير عن الجِنّ و عالمْهم.

سِمِع الرّاجِل العجوز قِصّة التّاجِر و قرّر إنُّه يِساعْدُه. راحوا سَوا لِمكان

الشّجرة اللي كان الجنّي مِسْتنّيهُم عندها.

قال الرّاجِل العجوز لِلْجنّي: "أنا عايِز أحْكيلك قِصّة قبْل ما تْقرّر مصير التّاجِر ده. لَوْ عجبتك القِصّة، أتمنّى إنّك تسامْحُه و تِسيبُه يِعيش."

وافِق الجنّي إنّه يِسْمع القِصّة. بدأ الرّاجِل العجوز يِحْكي قِصّة شيِّقة عن المُغامْرة و الشّجاعة و التّضْحية. كانِت القِصّة ملْيانة تشْويق و دُروس مُهمّة.

بعْد ما سِمِع الجنّي القِصّة، قال: "القِصّة عجبِتْني جِدّاً و اِتْعلّمْت مِنها دُروس هايْلة. أنا هسامِح التّاجِر و مِش هقْتِلُه، بِشرْط إنُّه يِخلّي بالُه و مَيْكرّرْش الغلْطة دي تاني."

شكر التّاجِر الجنّي على رحْمتُه، و وعد إنُّه هَياخُد بالُه مِن تصرُّفاتُه. و كمان شكر الرّاجِل العجوز على مُساعْدِتُه و حِكْمِتُه. بعْد كِده، رِجِع التّاجِر لِقرْيِتُه و أُسْرِتُه و وعد إنُّه هَيْكون حريص و عطوف أكْتر و هُوَّ بِيِتْعامِل معَ الطّبيعة و مخْلوقاتْها.

في اللّيْلة اللي بعْدها، خلّصِت شهْرزاد قِصّةْ التّاجِر و الجِنّي. كان الملِك شهْرَيار مبْهور بِالْقِصّة دي و كان عايِز يِسْمع كمان و كمان مِن القِصص الرّائِعة اللي شهْرزاد بِتِحْكيها. و بْكِده، فِضْلِت شهْرزاد تِحْكي قِصصْها لِلْملِك ليْلة بعْد ليْلة، و علِّمِت الملِك و شعْبُه دُروس مُهِمّة عن الحَياة و الحِكْمة و العدْل.

Questions

1. أيْه القِصّة اللي ابْتدِت شهْرزاد تِحْكيْها في اللّيْلة التّانيْة؟

2. ليْه الجِنّي غضب مِن التّاجِر؟

3. أيْه اللي الجِنّي طلب مِن التّاجِر يِعْمِلهُ عشان يِسامْحُه؟

4. مين الشّخْص اللي التّاجِر لقاه عشان يِساعْدُه؟

5. إزّاي الرّاجِل العجوز أقْنع الجِنّي إنُّه مَيِقْتِلْش التّاجِر؟

Answers

1. اِبْتِدِت شهْرزاد تِحْكي قِصّةْ التّاجِر و الجِنّي العجيب.

2. غضب الجِنّي عشان التّاجِر دمّر بيْتُه.

3. طلب الجِنّي مِن التّاجِر إنُّه يِجيب حدّ يِقْنِعُه إنُّه مَيِقْتلوش.

4. التّاجِر لقى راجِل عجوز حكيم كان بِعْرف حاجات كِتير عن الجِنّ و عالمْهُم.

5. أقْنع الرّاجِل العجوز الجِنّي إنُّه مَيِقْتِلْش التّاجِر عن طريق إنُّه حكاله قِصّة مُشوّقة عن المُغامْرة و الشّجاعة و التّضْحية، و بعْد ما الجِنّي سِمِع القِصّة، وافِق إنُّه يِسامِح التّاجِر و يْسيبُه يِعيش بِشرْط إنُّه ياخُد بالُه و مَيْكرّرْش الغلْطة دي تاني.

Chapter 2: The Genie and the Merchant

On the following night, King Shahryar asked Scheherazade to tell him a new story. Scheherazade began to narrate the tale of the merchant and the marvelous genie.

One day, a wealthy merchant went on a long journey to sell his goods. After a tiring journey, he stopped to rest under a tree. While he was sitting there, a giant and angry genie appeared.

The genie said to the merchant, "I will kill you because you destroyed my home." The merchant was frightened and did not understand what the genie meant. He asked the genie to explain the reason for his anger.

When you came and removed this wooden log to sit on it, some things fell on me and destroyed my small home where I lived.

The merchant was saddened by what had happened, but he did not know that there was a genie's home behind the tree. He asked the genie to show mercy and forgive him.

The genie said, "I will give you a chance to bring someone who can convince me not to kill you. If you fail, I will kill you for sure."

The merchant went on a long journey in search of someone to help him. Finally, he found a wise old man who knew a lot about genies and their world.

The old man listened to the merchant's story and decided to help him. They went together to the place of the tree where the genie was waiting for them.

The old man said to the genie, "I want to tell you a story before you decide the fate of this merchant. If you like the story, I hope you will forgive him and let him live."

The genie agreed to hear the story. The old man began to narrate an exciting tale of adventure, bravery, and sacrifice. The story was full of suspense and important lessons.

After hearing the story, the genie said, "I really liked the story and learned great lessons from it. I will forgive the merchant on the condition that he would be careful not to repeat such a mistake in the future."

The merchant thanked the genie for his mercy and promised to be more careful and compassionate in his actions. He also thanked the old man for his help and wisdom. Then, the merchant returned to his village and family and pledged to be more cautious and compassionate in his dealings with nature and its creatures.

On the following night, Scheherazade finished narrating the tale of the merchant and the genie. King Shahryar was impressed by this story and wanted to hear more wonderful stories told by Scheherazade. Thus, Scheherazade continued to narrate her stories to the king night after night, teaching him and his people important lessons about life, wisdom, and justice.

Questions
1. What is the story Scheherazade began to tell on the second night?
2. Why was the genie angry with the merchant?
3. What did the genie ask the merchant to do to forgive him?
4. Who did the merchant find to help him?
5. How did the old man convince the genie not to kill the merchant?

Answers
1. Scheherazade began to tell the story of the merchant and the strange genie.
2. The genie was angry because the merchant destroyed his home.
3. The genie asked the merchant to bring someone who could convince the genie not to kill him.
4. The merchant found a wise old man who knew a lot about genie and their world to help him.
5. The old man convinced the genie not to kill the merchant by telling an exciting story of adventure, bravery, and sacrifice. After hearing the story, the genie agreed to spare the merchant's life on the condition that he would be careful not to repeat such a mistake in the future.

الفَصْل التّالِت
الصّيّاد و السّمكة الذّهبية

في اللّيْلة اللي بعْدها، بدأتِ شهْرزاد تِحْكي قِصِّةْ السّمكة الذّهبية و الصّيّاد لِلْملِك شهْرَيار.

كان فيه صيّاد فقير عايِش في قرْيَة بسيطة على البحْر معَ مِراتُه. كان بيِصْطاد السّمك كُلّ يوْم عشان يِصْرِف على أُسْرتُه. و في يوْم مِن

الأيّام، اِصْطاد سمكة ذهبية حِلْوَة جِدّاً كانِت بِتِلْمع مِن كُتْر جمالْها. كلِّمتُه السَّمكة و قالتْلُه: "أنا سمكة سِحْرية، و لَوْ سِبْتني أنا هقْدر أحقّقْلك تلات أُمْنيّات تُطْلُبْهُم."

فكّر الصّيّاد في الحاجات اللي هُوَّ مِحْتاجْها و قرّر إنُّه يُطْلُب مِن السَّمكة الذَّهبية تِدّيلُه الثَّرْوَة و السَّعادة و الصِّحّة. ساب السَّمكة الذَّهبية و اِتْحقّقِت أُمْنيّاتُه.

حَياةُ الصّيّاد و مِراتُه اِتْحسّنِت جِدّاً بِفضْل الأُمْنيّات اللي حقّقِتْهالْهُم السَّمكة الذَّهبية. بسّ مَعَ مُرور الوَقْت، بدأِت مِراتُه تِطْمع في حاجات أكْتر، و طلبِت مِن جوزْها إنُّه يِرْجع للسَّمكة الذَّهبية علشان يُطْلُب أُمْنيّات كمان.

رِجع الصّيّاد للشّطّ، مكان ما صاد السَّمكة الذَّهبية، و ناداها. ظهرِت السَّمكة الذَّهبية تاني و سِمْعِت طلبات الصّيّاد. بسّ المرّة دي، حذّرِتُه السَّمكة الذَّهبية إنّ الطَّمع مِش هَيْجيبْلُهُم السَّعادة و الرَّاحة.

اِتْعلِّم الصّيّاد و مْراتُه الدّرْس المُهِمّ اللي السّمكة الذّهبية حبِّت تِعلِّمْهولْهُم، و قرّروا إنُّهُم يِكْتِفوا باللي معاهُم، و يِعيشوا حَياة بسيطة و سعيدة مِن غيْر طمع.

خلّصِت شهْرزاد قِصِّةْ السّمكة الذّهبية و الصّيّاد. كان الملِك شهْرَيار مُعْجب بالْقِصّة دي و كان عايِز يِسْمع قِصص أكْتر فيها دُروس قيِّمة و عِبر مُهِمّة. و بِالطّريقة دي، فِضْلِت شهْرزاد تِحْكي قِصصْها لِلْملِك شهْرَيار ليْلة بعْد ليْلة، و علِّمِتُه هُوَّ و شعْبُه دُروس مُهِمّة عن الرِّضا و التّواضُع و السّعادة.

Questions

1. أيْه القِصّة اللي ابْتدِت شهْرزاد تِحْكيها في اللّيْلة السّابْعة؟

2. أيْه اللي اصْطادُه الصّيّاد في يوْم حظُّه؟

3. أيْه اللي قالِتُه السّمكة الذّهبية للصّيّاد؟

4. أيْه الأُمْنِيّات اللي طلبْها الصّيّاد مِن السّمكة الذّهبية؟

5. إزّاي الصّيّاد و مْراتُه اِتْعلِّموا الدّرْس القيِّم اللي كانِت السّمكة الذّهبية عايْزة تِعلِّمْهولْهُم؟

Answers

1. اِبْتدِت شهْرزاد تِحْكي قِصّةْ السّمكة الذّهبية و الصّيّاد.

2. اِصْطاد الصّيّاد سمكة ذهبية جميلة كانِت بِتِلْمع مِن كُتْر جمالْها.

3. قالِت السّمكة الذّهبية للصّيّاد إنّها سمكة سِحْرية، و إنُّه لَوْ سابْها هتْحقّقْلُه تلات أُمْنِيّات هُوَّ عايزْها.

4. طلب الصّيّاد مِن السّمكة الذّهبية تدّيلُه الثّرْوَة و السّعادة و الصِّحّة.

5. حذّرِت السّمكة الذّهبية الصّيّاد و مْراتُه مِن إنّ الطّمع مِش هَيْجيبْلُهُم السّعادة و الرّاحة، اِتْعلِّم الصّيّاد و مْراتُه الدّرْس المُهِمّ و قرّروا إنُّهُم يِكْتِفوا بِاللى عِنْدُهُم و يِعيشوا حَياة بسيطة و سعيدة مِن غيْر طمع.

Chapter 3: The Fisherman and the Golden Fish

On the following night, Scheherazade began to tell the story of the Golden Fish and the Fisherman to King Shahryar.

There was a poor fisherman who lived in a simple coastal village with his wife. He fished every day to provide for his family. One day, he caught a beautiful golden fish that shimmered with brilliance and beauty. The fish spoke to him, saying, "I am a magical fish, and if you release me, I will grant you three wishes."

The fisherman thought about what he needed and decided to ask the golden fish to grant him wealth, happiness, and good health. He released the golden fish, and his wishes came true. The life of the fisherman and his wife improved greatly thanks to the wishes granted by the golden fish. But over time, his wife became greedy and asked her husband to return to the golden fish to ask for more wishes.

The fisherman returned to the beach, where he caught the golden fish and called out to it. The golden fish appeared again and listened to the fisherman's requests. But this time, the golden fish warned him that greed would not bring them happiness and peace.

The fisherman and his wife learned the valuable lesson that the golden fish wanted to teach them, and they decided to be content with what they had and live a simple and happy life without greed.

Scheherazade finished telling the story of the Golden Fish and the Fisherman. King Shahryar was impressed by this story and wanted to hear more stories that carry valuable lessons and important morals. In this way, Scheherazade continued to tell her stories to King Shahryar night after night, teaching him and his people important lessons about contentment, humility, and happiness.

Questions
1. What story did Scheherazade begin telling on the seventh night?
2. What did the fisherman catch on his lucky day?
3. What did the golden fish say to the fisherman?
4. What wishes did the fisherman ask the golden fish to grant him?
5. How did the fisherman and his wife learn the valuable lesson that the golden fish wanted to teach them?

Answers
1. Scheherazade began telling the story of the golden fish and the fisherman.
2. The fisherman caught a beautiful golden fish that sparkled with radiance and beauty.
3. The golden fish told the fisherman that it was a magical fish, and if he released it, it would grant him three wishes that he desired.

4. The fisherman asked the golden fish to grant him wealth, happiness, and good health.
5. The golden fish warned the fisherman and his wife that greed would not bring them happiness and peace. The fisherman and his wife learned a valuable lesson and decided to be content with what they had and live a simple and happy life without greed.

الفَصْل الرّابِع
علاء الدّين و المِصْباح السِّحْري

في اللّيْلة اللي بعْدها، بدإت شهْرزاد تِحْكي قِصِّةْ علاء الدّين و المِصْباح السِّحْري لِلْملِك شهْرَيار.

كان علاء الدّين وَلد فقير عايِش في مدينة صُغيّرة معَ والْدِتُه. في يوْم مِن الأيّام، قابِل راجِل غريب قالّه إنُّه عمُّه و عرض عليْه مُغامْرة

هَيْدَوّروا فيها على كِنْز مدْفون. على الرّغْم مِن شُكوك علاء الدّين، قرّر إنّه يِنْضمّ للرّاجِل الغريب في رِحْلتُه.

وَصلوا لِمغارة ضلْمة، الكِنْز كان مخْفي فيها. طلب الرّاجِل الغريب مِن علاء الدّين يِدْخُل المغارة و ياخُد مِصْباح قديم كان مَوْجود هِناك. بسّ بِمُجرّد ما علاء الدّين مِسِك المِصْباح، قفل الرّاجِل الغريب المغارة و سابُه محْبوس جوّاها.

في مُحاوْلة علشان يُخْرُج مِن المغارة، بدأ علاء الدّين يِدوّر على طريق الخُروج. لِقِي المِصْباح القديم و فكّر إنُّه مُمْكِن يِنوّر بيه المغارة الضّلْمة و يِدوّر على المخْرج. بدأ علاء الدّين يِمْسح التُّراب مِن على المِصْباح، و فجْأة ظهر جِنّي عِمْلاق. قال الجِنّي: "أنا جِنّي المِصْباح السِّحْري، و أنا هِنا عشان أحقّق تلات أُمْنِيّات تُطْلُبها."

بِمُساعْدةْ الجِنّي، قِدِر علاء الدّين يِهْرب مِن المغارة و رِجِع لِلْمدينة.

طلب مِن الجِنّي يِحقّق أُمْنِيّاتُه: إنُّه يِبْقى غني، و يِتجوِّز الأميرة و يِبْقى سُلْطان المدينة.

كُلّ أُمْنِيّات علاء الدّين اِتْحقّقِت، و بقى غني و اِتْجوِّز الأميرة و اِتْولّى حُكْم المدينة و بقى السُلْطان. بسّ الرّاجِل الغريب اللي كان بيِدّعي إنُّه عمُّه كان بيْخطّط علشان يِسْرق المِصْباح السِّحْري و يِسْتخْدِم قُوّتُه عشان بِتْحكّم في المدينة.

في يوْم مِن الأيّام، قِدِر الرّاجِل الغريب يِسْرق المِصْباح، و طلب مِن الجِنّي إنُّه يِنْقِل القصْر اللي كان علاء الدّين و الأميرة عايشْين فيه لِبلد بِعيدة. حسّ علاء الدّين بِاليأس، بسّ اِفْتكر خاتِم سِحْري كان الرّاجِل الغريب إدّاهولُه قبْل ما يِدْخُل المغارة.

اِسْتخْدم علاء الدّين الخاتِم السِّحْري عشان يِسْتدْعي جِنّي تاني كان بيِخْدِمُه. طلب مِن الجِنّي إنُّه يِنْقِلُه لِلْقصْر و يِرجّعُه لِلْمدينة. بِمُساعْدة الجِنّي و الأميرة، قِدِر علاء الدّين يِسْترْجِع المِصْباح السِّحْري و يِهْزِم الرّاجِل الغريب.

رِجِع علاء الدّين لِحَياتُه كسُلْطان، و عاش سعيد معَ الأميرة. اِتْعلّم علاء الدّين دُروس كِتيرة عن الثِّقة و الشّجاعة و الحُبّ.

خلّصِت شهْرزاد قِصّةْ علاء الدّين و المِصْباح السِّحْري. كان الملِك شهْرَيار مُعْجب بِالْقِصّة دي و كان عايِز يِسْمع كمان قِصص مُلْهِمة و مُثيرة. و كِده، فِضْلِت شهْرزاد تِحْكي قِصصْها لِلْملِك شهْرَيار كُلّ ليْلة، و تِعلّمُه هُوَّ و شعْبُه دُروس مُهِمّة عن الحَياة و الحِكْمة و العدْل..

Questions

1. أيْه القِصّة اللي شهْرزاد بدإِت تِحْكيها في اللّيْلة الرّابْعة؟

2. أيْه اللي عرضُه الرّاجِل الغريب على علاء الدّين؟

3. أيْه اللي لِقيه علاء الدّين جُوّه المغارة؟

4. أيْه اللي عملهُ الجِنّي اللي طِلِع مِن المِصْباح السِّحْري؟

5. أيْه الدُّروس اللي اتْعلِّمْها علاء الدّين مِن القِصّة دي؟

Answers

1. بدإت شهْرزاد تِحْكي قِصِّةْ علاء الدّين و المِصْباح السِّحْري.

2. عرض الرّاجِل الغريب على علاء الدّين مُغامْرة يِدوّروا فيها على كِنْز مدْفون.

3. لِقِي علاء الدّين مِصْباح قديم جُوّه المغارة.

4. قال الجِنّي إنُّه جاهِز عشان يِحقّق تلات أُمْنِيّات يُطْلُبْها علاء الدّين.

5. اِتْعلِّم علاء الدّين دُروس كِتير عن الثِّقة و الشّجاعة و الحُبّ.

Chapter 4: Aladdin and the Magic Lamp

On the next night, Scheherazade began to tell the story of Aladdin and the Magic Lamp to King Shahryar.

Aladdin was a poor boy who lived in a small city with his mother. One day, he met a strange man who claimed to be his uncle and offered him an adventure to search for a buried treasure. Despite Aladdin's suspicions, he decided to join the stranger on his journey.

They arrived at a dark cave where the treasure was hidden. The strange man asked Aladdin to enter the cave and take an old lamp that was there. But as soon as Aladdin got the lamp, the strange man closed the cave, trapping him inside.

In an attempt to get out of the cave, Aladdin started looking for a way out. He found the old lamp and thought it might be useful to light up the dark cave and to search for the exit. Aladdin started to wipe the dust off the lamp, and suddenly a giant genie appeared. The genie said, "I am the genie of the magic lamp, and I am here to grant three wishes that you make."

With the genie's help, Aladdin was able to escape from the cave and return to the city. He asked the genie to grant his wishes: to become rich, to marry the princess, and to become the sultan of the city.

All of Aladdin's wishes came true, and he became rich, married the princess, and became the sultan of the city. But the strange man who claimed to be his uncle was planning to steal the magic lamp and use its power to control the city.

One day, the strange man was able to steal the lamp and asked the genie to transport the palace where Aladdin and the princess lived to a distant land. Aladdin felt hopeless, but he remembered a magical ring that the strange man had given him before entering the cave.

Aladdin used the magical ring to summon another genie who served him. He asked the genie to transport him to the palace and return him to the city. With the help of the genie and the princess, Aladdin was able to retrieve the magic lamp and defeat the strange man.

Aladdin returned to his life as a sultan and lived happily with the princess. He learned many lessons about trust, courage, and love.

Scheherazade finished telling the story of Aladdin and the Magic Lamp. King Shahryar was impressed by this story and wanted to hear more inspiring and exciting stories. And so, Scheherazade continued to tell her stories to King Shahryar night after night, teaching him and his people important lessons about life, wisdom, and justice.

Questions
1. What story did Scheherazade begin telling on the fourth night?
2. What did the strange man offer Aladdin?
3. What did Aladdin find inside the cave?
4. What did the genie that came out of the magic lamp do?
5. What lessons did Aladdin learn from this story?

Answers
1. Scheherazade began telling the story of Aladdin and the Magic Lamp to King Shahryar.
2. The strange man offered Aladdin an adventure to search for a buried treasure.
3. Aladdin found an old lamp inside the cave.
4. The genie said he was there to grant three wishes that Aladdin requested.
5. Aladdin learned many lessons about trust, courage, and love.

الفصْل الخامِس
علي بابا و الأرْبعين حرامي

في اللّيْلة اللي بعْدها، بدأِت شهْرزاد تِحْكي لِلْملِك شهْرَيار قِصّةْ علي بابا و الأرْبعين حرامي.

علي بابا كان راجِل بسيط عايِش في قرْيَة صُغيّرة و كان بيِشْتغل حطّاب. في يوْم مِن الأيّام، و هُوَّ بِيقطّع الحطب في الغابة، شاف

مجْموعة مِن الحرامية بيدْخُلوا مغارة مخْفية. قال زعيم الحرامية كلِمة سرِّية: "افْتح يا سِمْسِم"، اتْفتحِت البوّابة الصخْرية و دخل الحرامية.

بعْد ما طِلع الحرامية مِن المغارة، راح علي بابا و قال الكلِمة السِّرِّية عشان يدْخُل المغارة. لِقي الكِنْز اللي الحرامية كانوا جمعوه و قرّر إنّه ياخُد جُزْء مِنُه عشان يساعِد أهْلُه و جيرانُه.

عِرْفِت مُرْجانة، الخدّامة الوَفية لِعلي بابا، سِرّ الكِنْز و مغارةْ الحرامية. لمّا زعيم الحرامية عِرِف إنّ علي بابا اِكْتشف سِرُّهُم، قرّر إنّه يِنْتِقِم مِنُّه و يْرجّع الكِنْز المسْروق.

قاوْمِت مُرْجانة مُحاوْلات الحرامية إنّهُم يِقْتِلوا علي بابا و أُسْرتِه، لِحدّ ما قِدْرِت في الآخِر تِقْتِل زعيم الحرامية و تِنْقِذ علي بابا. اِسْتخدم علي بابا جُزْء مِن الكِنْز عشان يِحسِّن حَياتُه هُوَّ و أُسْرتِه و يِساعِد الفُقرا و المِحْتاجين في القرْيَة.

خلّصِت شهْرزاد قِصِّةْ علي بابا و الأرْبعين حرامي. كان الملِك شهْرَيار مبْهور بِالْقِصّة و كان عايِز يِسْمع قِصص كمان فيها دُروس قيِّمة و عِبر مُهِمّة. و بِالطّريقة دي، فِضْلِت شهْرزاد تِحْكي قِصصْها لِلْملِك شهْرَيار كُلّ ليْلة، و تْعلِّمُه هُوَّ و شعْبُه دُروس مُهِمّة عن الحَياة و الشَّجاعة و الصَّداقة.

Questions

1. أيْه القِصّة اللي بدأِت شهْرزاد تِحْكيها في اللّيْلة الخامْسة؟

2. أيْه المِهْنة اللي كان علي بابا بيِشْتغلْها؟

3. أيْه الكِلْمة السِّرّية اللي اسْتخْدِمْها زعيم الحرامية عشان يِفْتح بوّابِةْ المغارة؟

4. مين مُرْجانة و أيْه دورْها في القِصّة؟

5. عمل أيْه علي بابا بِالْكِنْز اللي لقاه في المغارة؟

Answers

1. بدإِت شهْرزاد تِحْكي قِصّةْ علي بابا و الأربعين حرامي.

2. علي بابا كان بِيِشْتغل حطّاب.

3. الكِلْمة السِّرية اللي اسْتخْدِمْها زعيم الحرامية كانِت "افْتح يا سِمْسِم".

4. مُرْجانة هِيَّ الخدّامة الوَفية لِعلي بابا، عِرْفِت سِرّ الكِنْز و مغارةْ الحرامية، و قاوْمِت مُحاوْلات الحرامية إنُّهُم يِقْتِلوا علي بابا و أُسْرِتهْ، و في الآخِر قِدْرِت تِقْتِل زعيم الحرامية و تِنْقِذ علي بابا.

5. اِسْتخْدِم علي بابا جُزْء مِن الكِنْز عشان يِحسَّن حَياتُه هُوَّ و أُسْرِتهْ و يِساعِد الفُقرا و المِحْتاجين في القرْيَة.

Chapter 5: Ali Baba and the Forty Thieves

On the next night, Scheherazade began to tell the story of Ali Baba and the Forty Thieves to King Shahryar.

Ali Baba was a simple man who lived in a small village and worked as a woodcutter. One day while he was working in the forest, he saw a group of thieves entering a hidden cave. The leader of the thieves said a secret word, "Open Sesame," and the rock gate opened for them to enter.

After the thieves left the cave, Ali Baba went to the cave and said the secret word, entering the cave. He found the treasure that the thieves had collected and decided to take part of it to help his family and neighbors.

Morgiana, Ali Baba's loyal servant, learned about the treasure and the cave of the thieves. When the leader of the thieves learned that Ali Baba had discovered their secret, he decided to take revenge on him and get back the stolen treasure.

Morgiana fought against the attempts of the thieves to kill Ali Baba and his family until she finally managed to kill the leader of the thieves and save Ali Baba. Ali Baba used a part of the treasure to live a better life with his family and help the poor and needy in the village.

Scheherazade finished telling the story of Ali Baba and the Forty Thieves. King Shahryar was amazed by the story and wanted to hear more stories that carry valuable lessons and important messages. And so, Scheherazade continued to tell her stories to King Shahryar night after night, teaching him and his people important lessons about life, courage, and friendship.

Questions
1. What is the story that Scheherazade began to tell on the fifth night?
2. What was Ali Baba's profession?
3. What was the secret word used by the leader of the thieves to open the cave gate?
4. Who is Morgiana, and what was her role in the story?
5. What did Ali Baba do with the treasure he found in the cave?

Answers
1. Scheherazade began to tell the story of Ali Baba and the Forty Thieves.
2. Ali Baba worked as a woodcutter.
3. The secret word used by the leader of the thieves was "Open Sesame."
4. Morgiana was Ali Baba's loyal servant. She discovered the secret of the treasure and the thieves' cave, and she foiled the attempts of the thieves to kill Ali Baba and his family. In the end, she managed to kill the leader of the thieves and save Ali Baba.
5. Ali Baba used part of the treasure to live a better life with his family and help the poor and needy in the village.

الفصْل السّادِس
الفلّاح الذّكي و الجِنّي الشّقي

في اللّيْلة السّادسة، بدإت شهْرزاد تحْكي قصِّةْ الفلّاح الذّكي و الجنّي الشّقي للْملِك شهْرَيار.

كان فيه فلّاح فقير بيِشْتغل و بيِتْعب علشان يِكْسِب لُقْمةْ عيْشُه. في يوْم مِن الأيّامِ، لِقي الفلّاح جرّة نحاس قديمة مدْفونة في الغيْط

بِتاعُه. قرَّر الفلّاح يِفْتح الجرّة علشان يِشوف أيْه جُوّاها.

لمّا فتح الجرّة، طِلِع مِنْها جِنّي عِمْلاق، كان عايِز يِنْتِقِم مِن الفلّاح علشان قلق نومْتُه الهادْيَة الطَّويلة. كان الجِنّي فاكِر إنّ الفلّاح هَيُطْلُب مِنُّه أُمْنية علشان يِحسَّن حَياتُه، بسّ الفلّاح كان ذكي و عمل خِطّة علشان يِتْعامِل معَ الجِنّي.

قال الفلّاح لِلْجِني إنُّه مِش مِصدّق إنُّه قَوي، و شايِف إنُّه مِش هَيِقْدر يِرْجع تاني لِلْجرّة. حسّ الجِنّي بِالْغضب و الإهانة، فا قرّر يِثْبِت لِلْفلّاح إنُّه قَوي و رِجِع لِلْجرّة على طول. لمّا رِجِع الجِنّي لِلْجرّة، قِفِل الفلّاح الغطا و هُوَّ مبْسوط.

وَعد الفلّاح الجِنّي إنُّه هَيْخرّجُه تاني لَوْ وَعدُه إنُّه ميْئْذيش حدّ و إنُّه يِساعِد الفلّاح و عيلْتُه. قِبِل الجِنّي الشُّروط و اِتْعاوِن معَ الفلّاح، و اِتْحسَّنِت حَياة الفلّاح و عيلْتُه بِفضل قُوَّة الجِنّي و ذكاء الفلّاح.

خلّصِت شهْرزاد قِصّةْ الفلّاح الذّكي و الجنّي الشّقي. كان الملِك شهْرَيار مُعْجب بِالْقِصّة دي و عايِز يِسْمع قِصص أكْتر فيها دُروس قيِّمة و عِبر مُهِمّة عن الذّكاء و المكْر و التّعاوُن بيْن البشر و الجِنّ.

Questions

1. أيْه القِصّة اللي بدأِت شهْرزاد تِحْكيها في اللّيْلة السّادْسة؟

2. أيْه اللي لِقيه الفلّاح في الغيْط بِتاعُه؟

3. أيْه اللي الجِنّي كان فاكرُه لمّا الفلّاح خرّجُه؟

4. أيْه الخِطّة اللي عملْها الفلّاح علشان يِتْعامِل معَ الجِنّي؟

5. إزّاي اِتْحسّنِت حَياةْ الفلّاح و عيلْتُه؟

Answers

1. بدأِت شهْرزاد تِحْكي قِصّةْ الفلّاح الذّكي و الجِنّي الشّقي.

2. لِقي الفلّاح جرّة نِحاس قديمة مدْفونة في غيْطُه.

3. كان الجِنّي فاكِر إنّ الفلّاح هَيُطْلُب مِنُّه أُمْنية علشان يِحسّن حَياتُه.

4. قال الفلّاح للْجِنّي إنُّه مِش مِصدّق إنُّه قَوي و شايِف إنُّه مِش هَيِقْدر يِرْجع تاني لِلْجرّة. حسّ الجِنّي بِالْغضب و الإهانة، فا قرّر يِثْبِت لِلْفلّاح إنُّه قَوي و رِجِع لِلْجرّة على طول. لمّا رِجِع الجِنّي لِلْجرّة، قِفِل الفلّاح الغطا و هُوَّ مبْسوط.

5. اِتحسّنِت حَياةْ الفلّاح و عيْلتُه بِفضل قُوّةْ الجِنّي و ذكاء الفلّاح، بعْد ما وَعدُه الجِنّي إنُّه مَيِئْذيش حدّ، و إنُّه بِساعِد الفلّاح و عيْلتُه.

Chapter 6: The Clever Farmer and the Mischievous Genie

On the sixth night, Scheherazade began to tell the story of the Clever Farmer and the Mischievous Genie to King Shahryar.

There was a poor farmer who worked hard to provide for his family. One day, he found an old copper vessel buried in his field. The farmer decided to open the vessel to see what was inside.

As soon as he opened the vessel, a giant genie emerged from it, seeking revenge on the farmer for interrupting his long slumber. The genie thought the farmer would ask for a wish to improve his life, but the farmer was clever and had a plan to deal with the genie.

The farmer told the genie that he did not believe in his power and did not think he could return to the vessel. The genie felt angry and humiliated, so he decided to prove his power to the farmer and immediately returned to the vessel. Once the genie was back in the vessel, the farmer closed the lid with joy.

The farmer promised to release the genie again if he promised not to harm anyone and to help the farmer and his family. The genie agreed to the conditions and cooperated with the farmer, and the life of the farmer and his family improved thanks to the genie's power and the farmer's cleverness.

Scheherazade finished telling the story of the Clever Farmer and the Mischievous Genie. King Shahryar was impressed by this story and wanted to hear more stories that carry valuable lessons and important morals about intelligence, cunning, and cooperation between humans and genies.

Questions
1. What is the story that Scheherazade began to tell on the sixth night?
2. What did the farmer find in his field?
3. What did the genie think when the farmer released him?
4. What was the plan the farmer had to deal with the genie?
5. How did the life of the farmer and his family improve?

Answers
1. Scheherazade began to tell the story of the Clever Farmer and the Mischievous Genie.
2. The farmer found an old brass vessel buried in his field.
3. The genie thought the farmer would ask for a wish to improve his life.
4. The farmer told the genie that he did not believe in his power and did not think he could return to the vessel. The genie felt angry and humiliated, so he decided to prove his power to the farmer and immediately

returned to the vessel. Once the genie was back in the vessel, the farmer closed the lid with joy.

5. The life of the farmer and his family improved thanks to the genie's power and the farmer's cleverness after the genie promised not to harm anyone and to help the farmer and his family.

الفصْل السّابع
حرامي إسْكِنْدِرية و رئيس الشُّرطة

في ليْلة مِن لَيالي شهْرزاد، اِبْتدِت تِحْكي عن قِصّةْ حرامي إسْكِنْدِرية و رئيس الشُّرطة.

في مدينةْ إسْكِنْدِرية الجميلة، كان فيه حرامي ذكى و ماهِر بِيِسْرِق مِن الأغْنِيا و يِوَزّع على الفُقرا. كُلّ النّاس كانوا بِيِتْكلِّموا عن الحرامي ده لإنّه

محدِّش قِدِر يمْسِكُه. قرّر رئيس الشُّرْطة إنُّه يمِسك الحرامي ده و يوَقَّف جرايمُه.

فكّر رئيس الشُّرْطة في خِطّة ذكيّة عشان يقْبض على الحرامي. انْتشرِت إشاعة عن كنْز كبير هَيتْنِقِل في المدينة. الإشاعة دي كانِت مُجرّد فخّ عشان يجْذِب الحرامي.

في اللّيْلة المُحدّدة، اسْتنّى رئيس الشُّرْطة و رِجّالتُه في كمين عشان يقْبضوا على الحرامي. و فِعْلاً، ظهر الحرامي و حاوِل يسْرق الكنْز الوَهْمي. هِجِم عليْه رئيس الشُّرْطة و رِجّالتُه و قبض عليْه.

لكِن الحرامي مسْتسْلِمْش بِسْهولة، قِدِر إنُّه يفِلِت مِن الحِصار و هِرِب في زُقاق ضلْمة. بدأِت مُطارْدة مُثيرة بيْن الحرامي و رئيس الشُّرْطة في المدينة. في الآخِر، نِجِح رئيس الشُّرْطة إنُّه يمْسِك الحرامي و قبض عليْه.

و رغْم إنّ رئيس الشُّرْطة قبض على الحرامي، لكِنُّه كان مُعْترِف بِذكاؤُه و شجاعْتُه. و في المحْكمة، قرّر القاضى إنُّه يِدّى الحرامي فُرْصة يِغيرّ حَياتُه بإنّه يِشْتغل عند رئيس الشُّرْطة عشان يِحارِب الجريمة.

و بْكِده انْتهِت قِصِّةْ حرامي إسْكِنْدِرية و رئيس الشُّرْطة، إللى علِّمِتْنا إنّ الذَّكاء و الشّجاعة مُمْكِن يُسْتخْدموا للْخير.

Questions

1. حرامي إسْكِنْدِرية كان بِيِعْمِل أيْه بعْد ما بِيِسْرق مِن الأغْنِيا؟

2. أيْه قرّر رئيس الشُّرْطة يِعْمِلهُ عشان يُقْبَض على الحرامي؟

3. أيْه حصل لمّا الحرامي حاوِل يِسْرق الكِنْز الوَهْمي؟

4. إزّاي الحرامي قِدِر يِهْرب مِن الحِصار؟

5. أيْه اللي قرّر القاضي يِعْمِلهُ لِلْحرامي بعْد ما اتْقبض عليْه؟

Answers

1. حرامي إسْكِنْدرية كان بِيْوَزّع اللي سرقُه مِن الأغْنِيا على الفُقرا.

2. قرّر رئيس الشُّرْطة إنُّه يعْمِل خِطّة ذكية عشان يُقْبُض على الحرامي، و هِيَّ نشر إشاعة عن كِنْز كبير هَيتْنِقِل في المدينة، و كانِت الإشاعة دي فخّ عشان يِجْذِب الحرامي.

3. لمّا الحرامي حاوِل يِسْرق الكِنْز الوَهْمي، هجم عليْه رئيس الشُّرْطة و رِجّالتُه و قبضوا عليْه.

4. قِدِر الحرامي يِهرب مِن الحِصار عن طريق إنُّه مِسْتسْلِمْش بِسْهولة و هِرِب في زُقاق ضلْمة.

5. قرّر القاضى يِدّي الحرامي فُرْصة يِغيرّ حَياتُه بإنُّه يِشْتغل عنْد رئيس الشُّرْطة عشان يِقاوِم الجريمة.

Chapter 7: The Thief of Alexandria and the Police Chief

During one of Shahrazad's nights, she began to tell the story of the Thief of Alexandria and the Police Chief.

In the beautiful city of Alexandria, there was a clever and skilled thief who stole from the rich and gave to the poor. Everyone was talking about this thief because no one could catch him. The police chief decided to catch this thief and put an end to his crimes.

The police chief thought of a clever plan to capture the thief. A rumor spread about a huge treasure that would be transported through the city. This rumor was just a trap to lure the thief.

On the designated night, the police chief and his men waited in ambush to catch the thief. And indeed, the thief appeared and tried to steal the imaginary treasure. The police chief pounced on him and caught him.

But the thief did not surrender easily. He managed to escape the grip and fled into one of the dark alleys. An exciting chase began between the thief and the police chief throughout the city. In the end, the police chief managed to catch the thief and arrested him.

Despite the arrest of the thief, the police chief recognized his intelligence and courage. In court, the judge decided to give the thief a chance to change his life and work under the police chief to fight crime.

And so, the story of the Thief of Alexandria and the Police Chief ended, teaching us that intelligence and courage can be used for good.

Questions
1. What did the Thief of Alexandria do after stealing from the rich?
2. What did the police chief decide to do to catch the thief?
3. What happened when the thief tried to steal the imaginary treasure?
4. How did the thief manage to escape the grip?
5. What did the judge decide about the thief after his arrest?

Answers
1. The Thief of Alexandria distributed what he stole from the rich to the poor.
2. The police chief decided on a clever plan to catch the thief, which was to spread a rumor about a huge treasure that would be transported through the city, considering this rumor a trap to lure the thief.
3. When the thief tried to steal the imaginary treasure, the police chief and his men pounced on him and caught him.

4. The thief managed to escape the grip by not surrendering easily and fleeing into one of the dark alleys.
5. The judge decided to give the thief a chance to change his life and work under the police chief to fight crime.

الفَصْل التّامِن
العُصْفور الأَزْرق

في اللّيْلة اللي بعْدها، بدإت شهْرزاد تِحْكي لِلْملِك شهْرَيار حِكايةْ العصْفور الأزْرق.

كان فيه عصْفور أزْرق نادِر و جميل عايِش في غابة سِحْرية بِعيدة. كان النّاس بيْقولوا إنّ العصْفور الأزْرق ده يِقْدر يِجيب السّعادة و الحظّ

السّعيد لِلّي يْلاقيه. فيه أميرة شابّة سِمْعِت عن العصْفور الأزْرق و قرّرِت تِدوّر عليْه عشان تِحقّق السّعادة لِمَمْلكِتْها و شعْبها.

بدأِت الأميرة رِحْلة طَويلة و مُغامْرة شيِّقة عشان تِدوّر على العصْفور الأزْرق. و في الرِّحْلة دي، قابلِت أصْدِقاء كِتير و حَيَوانات مُتعاوْنة ساعْدِتْها إنّها تِعدّي كُلّ الصّعوبات و التّحدِيّات.

بعْد سِلْسِلةْ طَويلة مِن التّحدِيّات و المُغامْرات، لقِت الأميرة العصْفور الأزْرق. بسّ بدل ما يِجيبْلها السّعادة على طول، علّمْها العصْفور الأزْرق إنّ السّعادة الحقيقية بِتيجي مِن الشُّغْل باِجْتِهاد، و مُواجْهةْ المشاكِل و التّحدِيّات بِشجاعة و عزيمة.

رِجْعِت الأميرة لِمَمْلكِتْها و قالِت لِشعْبها الحِكْمة القيّمة اللي اتْعلّمِتْها مِن العصْفور الأزْرق. اِتْحسّنِت حَياةْ النّاس في المملْكة و زادِت سعادتْهُم، و بْكِده حقّقِت الأميرة هدفها مِن خِلال الشُّغْل بِالاِجْتِهاد و

التّعاوُن معَ شعْبها بدل ما تِعْتِمِد على قُوى سِحْرية.

خلّصِت شهْرزاد حِكايِةْ العصْفور الأزْرق.

كان الملِك شهْرَيار مبْهور بِالْحِكايَة و عايِز يِسْمع قِصص أكْتر فيها دُروس قيِّمة و عِبر مُهِمّة. و بِالطّريقة دي، اِسْتمرِّت شهْرزاد في إنّها تِحْكي لِلْملِك شهْرَيار حِكايَة وَرا حِكايَة، و تِعلِّمُه هُوَّ و شعْبُه دُروس مُهِمّة عن الشُّغْل الجادّ و مُواجْهِةْ التَّحْديّات بِشجاعة و عزيمة.

Questions

1. أيْه هِيَّ القِصّة اللي بدإت شهْرزاد تِحْكيها في اللّيْلة التّامْنة؟

2. أيْه القُدْرة السِّحْرية اللي عِنْد العصْفور الأزْرق؟

3. ليْه قرّرِت الأميرة تِدوّر على العصْفور الأزْرق؟

4. أيْه الدّرْس المُهِمّ اللي اتْعلِّمِتُه الأميرة مِن العصْفور الأزْرق؟

5. إزّاي اِتْحسِّنِت حَياةْ النّاس في المملكة بعْد ما رِجْعِت الأميرة؟

Answers

1. بدإِت شهْرزاد تِحْكي قِصِّةْ العصْفور الأزْرق.

2. العصْفور الأزْرق بيِمْتِلك القُدْرة على إنّه يِخلّي النّاس سُعْداء و بيِْجيب الحظّ السّعيد للي يقْدر يِلاقيه.

3. قرّرِت الأميرة تِدوّر على العصْفور الأزْرق عشان تِحقّق السّعادة لِممْلكِتْها و شعْبها.

4. اِتْعلِّمِت الأميرة مِن العصْفور الأزْرق إنّ السّعادة الحقيقية بتِيجي مِن الشُّغْل بِاجْتِهاد و مُواجْهةْ المشاكِل و التّحدِيّات بِشجاعة و عزيمة.

5. اِتْحسِّنِت حَياةْ النّاس في المملكة و زادِت سعادتْهُمْ بعْد ما عرّفِت الأميرة شعْبها الدّرْس المُهِمّ اللي اتْعلِّمِتُه مِن العصْفور الأزْرق، و حقّقِت هدفْها مِن خِلال الشُّغْل بِاجْتِهاد و التّعاوُن معَ شعْبها بدل ما تِعتِْمِد على قُوى سِحْرية.

Chapter 8: The Blue Bird

On the following night, Scheherazade began telling the story of the Blue Bird to King Shahryar.

There was a rare and beautiful blue bird that lived in a distant magical forest. It was said that the blue bird had the ability to grant happiness and good luck to those who could find it. A young princess heard about the Blue Bird and decided to search for it to bring happiness to her kingdom and its people.

The princess embarked on a long and exciting adventure to find the Blue Bird. She met, on her journey, many friends and helpful animals who helped her overcome obstacles and challenges.

After a long series of challenges and adventures, the princess finally found the Blue Bird. But instead of giving her happiness directly, the Blue Bird taught her that true happiness comes from hard work and facing problems and challenges with courage and determination.

The princess returned to her kingdom and shared the valuable lesson she learned from the Blue Bird with her people. Their lives improved, and their happiness increased. The princess had achieved her goal through hard work and cooperation with her people instead of relying on magical powers.

Scheherazade finished telling the story of the Blue Bird. King Shahryar was amazed by the story and wanted to hear more stories that carry valuable lessons and important morals. And so, Scheherazade continued to tell her stories to King Shahryar night after night, teaching him and his people important lessons about hard work and facing challenges with courage and determination.

Questions
1. What story did Scheherazade begin telling on the eighth night?
2. What magical ability does the Blue Bird have?
3. Why did the princess decide to search for the Blue Bird?
4. What valuable lesson did the princess learn from the Blue Bird?
5. How did people's lives improve in the kingdom after the princess's return?

Answers
1. Scheherazade began telling the story of the Blue Bird.
2. The Blue Bird has the ability to grant happiness and good luck to those who can find it.
3. The princess decided to search for the Blue Bird to bring happiness to her kingdom and its people.
4. The princess learned from the Blue Bird that true happiness comes from hard work and facing problems and challenges with courage and determination.

5. People's lives in the kingdom improved, and their happiness increased after the princess shared the valuable lesson she learned from the Blue Bird and achieved her goal through hard work and cooperation with her people instead of relying on magical powers.

الفَصْل التّاسِع
البِنْت و السّاحِرة العجوزة

في اللّيْلة اللي بعْدها، بدإت شهْرزاد تِحْكي للْملِك شهْرَيار عن قِصّة البِنْت و السّاحِرة العجوزة.

كانِت فيه بِنْت شابّة عايْشة معَ أُمّها في قرْيَة صُغيّرة. كانِت البِنْت بتْعاني مِن الفقْر و الجوع. في يوْم مِن الأيّام، لاقِت سِتّ عجوزة

بِتْبيع وَرْد في السّوق. اِشْترِت البِنْت وَرْدة مِن السِّتّ العجوزة بالْفُلوس القُلَيِّلة اللي كانِت معاها.

ضِحْكِت السِّتّ العجوزة و شكرِت البِنْت على لُطْفها. قالِتْلها إنّها ساحِرة و عرضِت عليْها تِحقّقْلها أُمْنية واحْدة. فكّرِت البِنْت في اللي هِيَّ عايْزاه و قرّرِت تُطْلُب مِن السّاحِرة العجوزة تِدّيلْها القُدْرة على إنّها تِخلّي النّاس اللي حَواليْها مبْسوطين.

قِبْلِت السّاحِرة العجوزة إنّها تِدّي البِنْت الهِبة اللي طلبِتْها. بدإِت البِنْت تِسْتخْدِم القُدْرة دي عشان تِفرّح النّاس في قرْيِتْها. معَ الوَقْت، اِتْشهْرِت البِنْت و بقِت محْبوبة و الكُلّ بِيْقدّرْها.

خلّصِت شهْرزاد قِصَّةْ البِنْت و السّاحِرة العجوزة. كان الملِك شهْرَيار مُعْجب بالْقِصّة دي و حبّ يِسْمع قِصص تانْيَة فيها دُروس قيِّمة و عِبر مُهِمّة عن الإحْسان و التّفاني في خِدْمةْ النّاس. و بْكِده،

فِضْلِت شهْرزاد تِحْكي قِصصْها لِلْملِك شهْرَيار كُلّ ليْلة و تْعلِّمُه هُوَّ و شعْبُه دُروس مُهِمّة عن التّضْحية و التّفاني في مُساعْدةْ النّاس و تحْقيق السّعادة لِلْكُلّ.

Questions

1. أيه القِصّة اللي بدأِت شهْرزاد تِحْكيها في اللّيْلة التّاسْعة؟

2. أيه اللي كانِت السِّتّ العجوزة بِتْبيعُه في السّوق؟

3. أيه اللي طلبِتُه البِنْت مِن السّاحِرة العجوزة؟

4. إزّاي الهِبة اللي السّاحِرة العجوزة إدّتْها لِلْبِنْت أثّرِت على حَياتْها؟

5. أيه الدُّروس المُهِمّة اللي علّمِتْها شهْرزاد لِلْملِك شهْرَيار و شعْبُه مِن خِلال القِصّة دي؟

Answers

1. بدأِت شهْرزاد تِحْكي قِصّةْ البِنْت و السّاحِرة العجوزة.

2. السِّتّ العجوزة كانِت بِتْبيع وَرْد في السّوق.

3. طلبِت البِنْت مِن السّاحِرة العجوزة إنّها تِدّيها القُدْرة على إنّها تِخلّي النّاس اللي حَواليْها مبْسوطين.

4. بدإِت البِنْت تِسْتخْدِم القُدْرة دي عشان تِفرّح النّاس في قرْيِتْها، و معَ الوَقْت، اِتْشهرِت البِنْت و بقِت محْبوبة و الكُلّ بِيِقْدرْها.

5. علِّمِت شهْرزاد الملِك شهْرَيار و شعْبُه دُروس مُهِمّة عن التّضْحية و التّفاني في مُساعْدةْ النّاس و تحْقيق السّعادة لِلْكُلّ.

Chapter 9: The Girl and the Magical Old Woman

On the following night, Scheherazade began telling the story of the Girl and the Magical Old Woman to King Shahryar.

There was a young girl who lived with her mother in a small village. The girl suffered from poverty and hunger. One day, she stumbled upon an old woman selling flowers in the market. The girl bought a flower from the old woman with the little money she had.

The old woman smiled and thanked the girl for her kindness. She revealed that she was a sorceress and offered to grant the girl one wish. The girl thought about what she wanted and decided to ask the magical old woman to give her the ability to make people around her happy.

The magical old woman granted the girl the gift she asked for. The girl began using this ability to make people in her village happy. With time, the girl's fame spread, and she became beloved and honored by everyone.

Scheherazade finished telling the story of the Girl and the Magical Old Woman. King Shahryar was impressed by this story and wanted to hear stories that carried valuable lessons and important morals about kindness and dedication to serving others. And so, Scheherazade continued to tell her stories to King Shahryar night after night, teaching him and his people important lessons about generosity and selflessness to help others and achieve happiness for all.

Questions
1. What story did Scheherazade start telling on the ninth night?
2. What was the old woman selling in the market?
3. What did the girl ask the magical old woman for?
4. How did the gift given to the girl by the magical old woman affect her life?
5. What important lessons did Scheherazade teach King Shahryar and his people through this story?

Answers
1. Scheherazade started telling the story of the girl and the magical old woman.
2. The old woman was selling flowers in the market.
3. The girl asked the magical old woman to grant her the ability to make people around her happy.
4. The girl began using this ability to make people happy in her village, and over time, her fame spread, and she became loved and honored by everyone.
5. Scheherazade taught King Shahryar and his people important lessons about sacrifice and selflessness in helping others and achieving happiness for all.

الفَصْل العاشِر
الأمير و التِّنين

في اللَّيْلة اللي بعْدها، بدأِت شهْرزاد تِحْكي قِصِّة الأمير و التِّنين لِلْمِلك شهْرَيار.

كان فيه أمير شابّ و شُجاع عايِش في ممْلكة بعِيدة. اِنْتشر في البِلاد خبر إنّ فيه تِنين عِمْلاق عايِش في جبل قُرَيِّب، بيْهدِّد القُرى القُرَيِّبة و

بِيْخوِّف النَّاس. قرَّر الأمير إنُّه يواجِهْ التِّنين و يِنْقِذ شعْبُه مِن الخطر.

جهَّز الأمير نفْسُه لِلْمعْركة و اِتَّجهْ لِلْجبل. لمَّا قابِل الأمير التِّنين، اِكْتشف إنُّه مِش شِرِّير زيّ ما كان النَّاس فاكْرين. التِّنين كان بِيِتْسبَّب في التَّدْمير عشان كان حاسِس بِألم في جِسْمُه. عرض الأمير إنُّه يِساعِد التِّنين في عِلاج ألمُه بِشرْط إنُّه يِوْعِدُه مَيْضُرِّش النَّاس تاني.

وافِق التِّنين على الاِتِّفاق و الأمير ساعْدُه. بعْد ما التِّنين خفَّ، عاش هُوَّ و الأمير في سلام و صداقة، و اِتْعاوْنوا في حِمايةْ القُرى و البِلاد مِن الأعْداء و الخطر.

خلَّصِت شهْرزاد قِصَّةْ الأمير و التِّنين. كان الملِك شهْرَيار مبْهور بِالْقِصَّة، و حبّ يِسْمع قِصص أكْتر فيها دُروس قيِّمة و معاني مُهِمَّة عن الصَّداقة و التَّفاهُم بيْن المخلوقات المُخْتلِفة.

و بِكِده، فِضْلِت شهْرزاد تِحْكي قِصصْها اللي مليانة عِبر و حِكم لِلْمِلك شهْرَيار كُلّ ليْلة. اِتْأثّر الملِك جِدّاً بِكلام شهْرزاد و دُروسْها القيِّمة، و اِتْغيّرِت نظْرِتُه لِلْحَياة و العالم حَواليْه.

و بِفضْل حِكْمِةْ شهْرزاد و قُدْرِتْها على التّواصُل و نقْل العِبر و الدُّروس القيِّمة عن طريق قِصصْها، الملِك شهْرَيار بقى ملِك حكيم و عادِل. رجّع السّلام و النّجاح لِممْلكتُه و حكم بِحِكْمة و رحْمة مشافْهُمْش الشّعْب قبْل كِده.

بِمُرور الزّمن، اِكْتشف الملِك شهْرَيار إنُّه لِقي في شهْرزاد الزّوْجة الحكيمة و المُخْلِصة. بقِت شهْرزاد ملِكة محبوبة مِن الشّعْب و أُمّ لِلأميرة الصُّغيّرة.

فِضْلِت شهْرزاد تِحْكي القِصص لِلمِلك كُلّ ليْلة، و ده خلّاه يْقدّرْها و يِحْتِرِمْها أكْتر و أكْتر. و عاش الملِك شهْرَيار و شهْرزاد سُعْداء معَ بعْض، و فِضْلِت قِصصْها تْنشُر الحِكْمة و المعْرِفة في كُلّ الممْلكة.

و بِكِده، اِسْتمرِّت شهْرزاد في تأْليف قِصص مُثيرة و رائعة لِلْمِلك

شهْرَيار ليْلة بعْد ليْلة، و فِضْلوا يتْعلَّموا مِن دُروسْها و عجائبْها. اِسْتمرَّت المَمْلكة في الاِزْدِهار تحْتَ حِكْمةْ و سعادِةْ شهْرزاد و شهْرَيار، و بقِت قِصص ألْف ليْلة و ليلة مصْدر إلْهام لِلنّاس في كُلّ أنْحاء العالم.

Questions

1. أيْه القِصّة اللي شهْرزاد بدأِت تِحْكيها في اللّيْلة العاشْرة؟

2. أيْه هُوَّ الخبر اللي انْتشر عن التِّنين اللي عايِش في الجبل؟

3. أيْه اللي الأمير اِكْتشفُه لمّا قابِل التّنين؟

4. أيْه الاتِّفاق اللي الأمير عملُه معَ التّنين؟

5. إزّاي قِصص شهْرزاد أثّرِت على الملِك شهْرَيار و ممْلكْتُه؟

Answers

1. بدأِت شهْرزاد تِحْكي قِصّةْ الأمير و التّنين.

2. اِنْتشر خبر عن تِنين كِبير عايِش في جبل قُرَيِّب، بيْهدِّد القُرى القُرَيِّبة و يِخوِّف النّاس.

3. اِكْتشف الأمير إنّ التّنين مِش شِرِّير زيّ ما كان النّاس فاكرين، لكِن التّنين كان بيِتْسبِّب في التّدْمير عشان كان حاسِس بألم في جِسْمهُ.

4. عرض الأمير إنّهُ يِساعِد التّنين في عِلاج ألمهُ بِشرْط إنّهُ يِوْعِدهُ مَيْضرِّش النّاس تاني. و وافِق التّنين على الاِتِّفاق ده.

5. اِتْأثّر الملِك شهْرَيار بِشكْل عميق بِكلام شهْرزاد و عِبرها القيِّمة، و اِتْغيِّرِت نظْرتهُ لِلْحَياة و العالم مِن حَواليْه. بقى ملِك حكيم و عادِل و رجّع السّلام و الاِزْدِهار لِمَمْلكْتهُ. عِلِم شعْبهُ مِن العِبر و الدُّروس القيِّمة اللي مَوْجودة في قِصص شهْرزاد، و اِزْدهرِت المَمْلكة و عاش شعْبها في سلام و سعادة.

Chapter 10: The Prince and the Dragon

On the next night, Scheherazade began telling the story of the Prince and the Dragon to King Shahryar.

There was a young and brave prince who lived in a distant kingdom. News spread in the land about a huge dragon living in a nearby mountain, threatening the neighboring villages and scaring people. The prince decided to face the dragon and save his people from danger.

The prince prepared for the battle and headed to the mountain. When he faced the dragon, he discovered that the dragon was not evil as everyone thought. Rather, he caused destruction because of pain in his body. The prince offered to help the dragon to heal his pain in exchange for a promise not to harm people again.

The dragon agreed to the deal, and the prince helped him. After the dragon healed, the prince and the dragon lived in peace and friendship, and they cooperated to protect the villages and the country from enemies and risks.

Scheherazade finished narrating the story of the Prince and the Dragon. King Shahryar was impressed by this story and wanted to hear more stories that carry valuable lessons and important messages about friendship and understanding between different creatures.

And so, Scheherazade continued to tell her stories filled with lessons and wisdom to King Shahryar every night. King Shahryar was deeply affected by Scheherazade's words and valuable messages, and his view of life and the world around him changed.

Thanks to Scheherazade's wisdom and her ability to communicate and convey valuable lessons and messages through her stories, King Shahryar became a wise and just king. He restored peace and prosperity to his kingdom and ruled with wisdom and mercy that the people had not seen before.

Over time, King Shahryar realized that he had found in Scheherazade a wise and loyal wife. Scheherazade became a beloved queen to the people and a mother to the little princess.

Scheherazade continued to tell stories to the king every night, making him appreciate and respect her more and more. King Shahryar and Scheherazade lived happily together as her stories continued to spread wisdom and knowledge throughout the kingdom.

And thus, Scheherazade continued to weave her thrilling and wonderful stories for King Shahryar night after night, learning from them and teaching him with her lessons and marvels. The kingdom thrived under the wisdom and happiness of Scheherazade and Shahryar, while the tales of One Thousand and One Nights inspired people all over the world.

Questions
1. What was the story that Scheherazade began telling on the tenth night?
2. What rumor spread about the dragon living in the mountain?
3. What did the prince discover when he faced the dragon?
4. What agreement did the prince make with the dragon?
5. How did Scheherazade's stories affect King Shahryar and his kingdom?

Answers
1. Scheherazade began telling the story of the Prince and the Dragon.
2. Rumors spread in the land about a huge dragon living in a nearby mountain, threatening the neighboring villages and scaring people.
3. The prince discovered that the dragon was not evil as everyone thought. Rather, he caused destruction because of pain in his body.
4. The prince offered to help the dragon to heal his pain in exchange for a promise not to harm people again, and the dragon agreed to the agreement.
5. King Shahryar was deeply affected by Scheherazade's words and valuable messages, and his view of life and the world around him changed. He became a wise and just king who restored peace and prosperity to his

kingdom. The people learned from the lessons and valuable messages carried by Scheherazade's stories, and the kingdom prospered, and its people lived in peace and happiness.

lingualism

Visit our website for information on current and upcoming titles and free language learning resources.

www.lingualism.com

www.ingramcontent.com/pod-product-compliance
Lightning Source LLC
Chambersburg PA
CBHW062035120526
44592CB00036B/2146